THE WEAPONS ENCYCLOPÆDIA
TANK AIRCRAFT AFV SHIP ARTILLERY VEHICLES SECRET WEAPON

TWE-031 ENG

🇬🇧 UK AND OTHER M4 SHERMAN TANKS

THE WEAPONS ENCYCLOPAEDIA

EDITORIAL STAFF
Luca Cristini, Paolo Crippa.

ACADEMIC STAFF
Enrico Acerbi, Massimiliano Afiero, Aldo Antonicelli, Ruggero Calò, Luigi Carretta, Flavio Chistè, Anna Cristini, Carlo Cucut, Salvo Fagone, Enrico Finazzer, Arturo Giusti, Björn Huber, Andrea Lombardi, Aymeric Lopez, Marco Lucchetti, Gabriele Malavoglia, Luigi Manes, Giovanni Maressi, Francesco Mattesini, Daniele Notaro, Péter Mujzer, Federico Peirani, Alberto Peruffo, Maurizio Raggi, Andrea Alberto Tallillo, Antonio Tallillo, Roberto Vela, Massimo Zorza.

PUBLISHED BY
Luca Cristini Editore (Soldiershop), via Orio, 35/4 - 24050 Zanica (BG) ITALY.

DISTRIBUTION BY
Soldiershop - www.soldiershop.com, Amazon, Ingram Spark, Berliner Zinnfigurem (D), LaFeltrinelli, Mondadori, Libera Editorial (Spain), Google book (eBook), Kobo, (eBoook), Apple Book (eBook).

PUBLISHING'S NOTES
None of unpublished images or text of our book may be reproduced in any format without the expressed written permission of Luca Cristini Editore (already Soldiershop.com) when not indicate as marked with license creative commons 3.0 or 4.0. Luca Cristini Editore has made every reasonable effort to locate, contact and acknowledge rights holders and to correctly apply terms and conditions to Content. Every effort has been made to trace the copyright of all the photographs. If there are unintentional omissions, please contact the publisher in writing at: info@soldiershop.com, who will correct all subsequent editions.

LICENSES COMMONS
This book may utilize part of material marked with license creative commons 3.0 or 4.0 (CC BY 4.0), (CC BY-ND 4.0), (CC BY-SA 4.0) or (CC0 1.0). We give appropriate attribution credit and indicate if change were made in the acknowledgments field. Our WTW books series utilize only fonts licensed under the SIL Open Font License or other free use license.

CONTRIBUTORS OF THIS VOLUME & ACKNOWLEDGEMENTS
We thank the main contributors to this issue: The profiles of the floats are all by the author. Photo coloring is by Anna Cristini. Special thanks to national and/or private institutions such as: Army General Staff, State Archives, Bundesarchiv, Nara, Library of Congress, Wikipedia, USAF, Signal magazine, War Chronicles, War Front, IWM, Australian War Museum, etc. A P.Crippa, A.Lopez, Péter Mujzer, L.Manes, C.Cucut, Tallillo archives. Model Victoria (www.modelvictoria.it) etc. for making available images or other from their archives.

For a complete list of Soldiershop titles, or for every information please contact us on our website: www.soldiershop.com or www.cristinieditore.com. E-mail: info@soldiershop.com. Keep up to date on Facebook https://www.facebook.com/soldiershop.publishing

Title: **M4 SHERMAN MEDIUM TANK - UK & ALLIED M4 TANKS - VOL. II** Code.: TWE-031 EN
Series by Luca Stefano Cristini
ISBN code: 9791255891680 First edition November 2024
THE WEAPONS ENCYCLOPAEDIA (SOLDIERSHOP) is a trademark of Luca Cristini Editore

THE WEAPONS ENCYCLOPÆDIA
TANK AIRCRAFT AFV SHIP ARTILLERY VEHICLES SECRET WEAPON

M4 SHERMAN MEDIUM TANK
UK & ALLIED M4 TANKS - VOL. II

LUCA STEFANO CRISTINI

BOOK SERIES FOR MODELERS & COLLECTORS

CONTENTS

Introduction 5
   - Technical Characteristics 6
   - Models in British (and Commonwealth) use 11

Operational use 23
   - North African Front 23
   - Italy campaign of British forces 25
   - The Normandy landings and the French campaign 25
   - Sherman military interventions by other countries 29

Camouflage and distinctive markings 41
   - European and metropolitan theater coloration 41
   - Middle Eastern and African theater coloration 42
   - Far Eastern theater coloration 42
   - Camouflage specifications and markings 47

Appendix 52

Data Sheets 52

Bibliography 58

▼ British tank sergeant A.G. Williams of the 17th/21st Lancers in the turret of his Sherman deployed at San Angelo in Italy in April 1944.

INTRODUCTION

Considered to be one of the most significant tanks of the Second World War, especially due to the large number produced, the American M4 soon became the backbone of the British armoured forces. After the defeat suffered by British and Commonwealth troops at Tobruk in June 1942, President Roosevelt pledged to supply sufficient tanks to the British ally. In addition, to help his ally as much as possible, Roosevelt also proposed to immediately send the American 2nd Armoured Division to North Africa. However, it was soon realised that this plan had critical aspects and was not feasible. The final decision was therefore to transfer the US tanks directly to the British 8th Army. Despite the logistical difficulties of transporting such a large number of tanks, further complicated by the sinking of a merchant ship loaded with tanks by a German U-boat, at least 250 Sherman tanks still managed to reach Egypt in time to be deployed in Operation Lightfoot - the Second Battle of El Alamein - in October 1942. In line with the British custom of renaming tanks, at Winston Churchill's suggestion, the new vehicle was named Sherman, without the need to add any prefix.

By the end of the conflict, the Sherman was mainly used as a medium tank, recovery vehicle and in various specialised roles. The original design had undergone numerous modifications, and total production reached tens of thousands of examples, built by more than a dozen companies. In this second volume, we

▲ The first Sherman sent to the British Army still shows the three 30mm machine guns mounted on the hull; the pair of fixed weapons was soon removed (1942).

will focus on the Shermans in service with British and Commonwealth forces, as well as Polish, French and Russian forces. The numerous specialised variants, such as cranes, engineer vehicles, self-propelled artillery vehicles or tank destroyers, based on the Sherman chassis, will not be covered. These will be the topics of the third and final volume dedicated to the Sherman!

■ TECHNICAL CHARACTERISTICS

Main armament:

- Cannon: 75 mm M3 (in early versions).

Munitions: High explosive (HE) and armour-piercing (AP) projectiles, with a muzzle velocity of approximately 620 m/s. The gun was effective against light armoured vehicles and for infantry support, but proved ineffective against German heavy tanks such as the Tiger and Panther.

- 76 mm M1 cannon, with a higher muzzle velocity (around 792 m/s) to cope with thicker armour.

Secondary armament:

- Co-axial machine gun: Browning M1919A4 7.62 mm (calibre .30).
- Hull gun: A second 7.62 mm Browning M1919A4 mounted in the front hull.
- Aircraft gun: Browning M2 12.7 mm (calibre .50) mounted on the turret for defence against enemy aircraft or infantry.

Armour plating:

- Thickness of the front armouring: Varies between 51 mm and 76 mm of cast or rolled steel.
- Lateral armouring: approx. 38 mm.

▲ British M4A1 column of the 1st Armoured Division at El Alamein, 24 October 1942.

UK Sherman III Medium Tank (M4A2), 2nd Armoured Brigade, Benghazi, Libya, December 1941.

▲ The British army in North Africa began to receive the first American tanks, absolutely necessary to contain and then defeat the Axis forces in that chessboard of the front. North Africa 1942.

The armour was sloped to improve protection, but it was still vulnerable to powerful German guns, especially the 88mm cannon.

Propulsion and Mobility:

Engine: Different engines were used depending on the variants. Initial versions were equipped with a Continental R975 C1 nine-cylinder, radial, air-cooled petrol engine with an output of around 400-450 hp. Later versions, such as the M4A3, were fitted with the more powerful 500 hp Ford GAA V8 petrol engine.

-Maximum speed: Approximately 38-48 km/h on the road, depending on the model and ground conditions.

-Autonomy: Approx. 160-240 km on the road with a full tank of fuel (approx. 660 litres of petrol).

Suspension:

-Vertical Volute Spring Suspension (VVSS): In early versions, they allowed decent mobility, but could be a little stiff on rough terrain.

-Horizontal Volute Spring Suspension (HVSS): In later versions (such as the M4A3E8 'Easy Eight'), the suspension was improved for better stability and ride comfort.

Dimensions and Weight:

-Length: approx. 5.84 m (with cannon included).

-Width: approx. 2.62 m.

-Height: approx. 2.74 m.

-Weight: Approx. 30-33 tonnes depending on model and modifications.

Crew:

Composed of five members:

-Commander

-Cannonier

-Servant

-Pilot

-Assistant pilot/radio operator

Ammunition:

-Capacity of carrying 90-97 projectiles for the main gun (75 mm or 76 mm).

-About 4,750 rounds for the 7.62 mm machine guns.

-300-500 rounds for the 12.7 mm anti-aircraft machine gun.

Communications:

-Equipped with an SCR 528 radio for internal and external communications on the battlefield.

▲ A beautiful picture of a British M4A2 in Tunisia, July 1943.

Medium tank UK Sherman Mk. II, 3rd King's Hussars, 5th Armoured Brigade, 8th Army, Egypt, September 1942.

MODELS IN BRITISH (AND COMMONWEALTH) USE

Below are the main characteristics of the models used by the British army, which, let us remember, received a different designation from the American one that began with M4 and other letters. The British named the Sherman tank, as they had already done with the M3 tank called Grant and Lee, with numbering increasing. Only those models actually used in combat are included in this list, not those for engineer and other purposes.

It should also be remembered that the British received a very large number of M4 medium tanks, over 17,000 units (about one in every three of the M4s produced), more than any other Allied nation.

Following their tradition of renaming American vehicles after American Civil War generals, the British renamed the M4 'Sherman,' in honour of Union General William Tecumseh Sherman. Later, the United States also adopted this convention and began using the name 'General Sherman' for the M4.

In the British classification system, the main models of the M4 were designated by progressive numbers: the basic M4 became 'Sherman I,' the M4A1 'Sherman II,' and so on. Additional letters after the number specified further modifications: the letter "A" denoted the 76 mm L/55 gun replacing the 75 mm, "B" designated the 105 mm M4 L/22.5 howitzer, "C" represented the British 76.2 mm QF 17-pounder gun, and "Y" identified the improved HVSS (Horizontal Volute Spring Suspension) with wider tracks.

Letters could be combined to signal specific configurations, such as "Sherman IBY." However, not all

▲ The Continental-Wright-9-Zylinder-Sternmotor R97 in its original harness is being mounted on a British Shermann M4A1. Normandy 1944.

Medium tank UK Sherman Mk. II, 9th Queen's Royal Lancers, El Alamein, Egypt, October 1942.

▲ Beautiful shot of a Canadian tank crew aboard their Sherman in June 1944 after the Normandy landings in the area of Vaucelles, Calvados. PD

Medium tank UK Sherman IIII, 'Cocky', 41st Battalion, Royal Tank Regiment, el Alamein, Egypt, October 1942.

combinations were present: for example, no 75 mm Sherman was built with HVSS; thus, there were no versions designated as 'CY' for the 17-pounder armament. HVSS-equipped Shermans in UK service mounted only 76 mm M1 guns or 105 mm M4 howitzers, identified as "AY" and "BY" respectively."

- **Sherman I (M4)**

This model was actually the third type of Sherman to be produced. All vehicles of this type were fitted with a 9-cylinder Wright petrol engine. The simple, welded hull was designed to facilitate production, while the turret was equipped with a 75mm M3 cannon and a 30mm machine gun. The front armour, sloping 60 degrees, featured square extensions that included hatches for the driver and gunner. The British were the first to test the tank in combat, quickly realising what modifications were necessary or possible. One of the first suggestions concerned the positioning of the radio, which the British moved from the hull structure to the turret, unlike the American designers. Other features, such as the suspension and gun mounts, were similar to those of the Sherman II and III. In the OP (observation post) version, used for command and reconnaissance, the main gun was removed and replaced with a wooden dummy gun to deceive the enemy. In the British Army, at least until D-Day, there was one OP tank for every 5-10 tanks with cannon.

- **Sherman I C**

This variant, equipped with a British 76.2 mm cannon, was identified by the suffix "C." Otherwise, it retained the same hull as the Sherman I.

- **Sherman Hybrid I**

This version, developed from the M4A1, was called 'hybrid' by the British. It featured a redesigned hull front, with a single cast front section and wider access hatches, while the rear was welded. This version only came into service after the Normandy landings. Again, the Hybrid IC version referred to the model equipped with a more powerful gun, the British 76.2 mm QF 17-pounder.

- **Sherman IB (M4 105)**

The Sherman IB model was an evolution of the Sherman I, characterised by a hull with 47-degree sloping armour, and was distinguished by the powerful 105 mm M4 L/22.5 howitzer, installed in a turret equipped with a 30 mm coaxial machine gun. For better visibility, the commander had a new observation dome. This model found extensive use in Italy from September 1944 onwards, proving very effective as a close support vehicle, often combined with command squadrons. The first deliveries took place in September 1944, with a total production of just under 170 units. A variant called the Sherman IBY was developed, equipped with HVSS suspension to improve mobility.

- **Sherman II (M4AI)**

The Sherman II was the first model of this series to be delivered to the British Army, becoming the most popular tank in the North African theatre. Armed with a 75 mm M3 L/40 cannon and powered by a Continental R975 petrol radial engine, it was a robust and reliable vehicle. Some versions, called Sherman IIA, were equipped with a slightly shorter 75 mm M2 cannon. As time went on, many examples were adapted as engineering support vehicles. The variant with HVSS suspension was known as the Sherman IIAY.

- **Sherman IIA (M4A1 76mm)**

This version, still equipped with a 76 mm cannon, introduced a new turret (T23) with a completely new design, as well as a more advanced observation dome for the commander. These improvements led to an increase in the overall weight of the vehicle. The Sherman IIA model was also used extensively by British forces in Italy, with deliveries starting in the winter of 1944 totalling over 500 units.

- **Sherman III (see page 52)**

Together with the Sherman II, the Sherman III was one of the main tanks used in the Battle of El Alamein, contributing significantly to the success of the British armoured force. The welded hull was similar to that of the Sherman I, but differed in its engine access doors, rear configuration and exhaust system. This tank, powered by a General Motors GM6046 diesel engine, was produced in over 5,000 units for the British Army, which dubbed it the 'Sherman Diesel' to distinguish it from the petrol-powered Sherman. The Sherman III's main theatre of operations was Italy, where the tank played a decisive role from the invasion of Sicily until the end of the war. Some examples also participated in the Normandy campaign, albeit in limited numbers.

In time, several Sherman IIIs were converted for armoured troop transport, taking the name 'Sherman Kangaroos'. A variant with a 76 mm M1A2 L/55 gun, called the Sherman IIIA, was also produced, but was not operationally adopted by British troops. The Sherman IIIAY version, equipped with HVSS suspension, also does not appear to have been used by the British.

- **Sherman IV**

This model, designated M4A3 in the United States, was armed with the M3 L/40 75 mm cannon. Its production was limited, and information on the operational assignment of these vehicles is scarce. However, it is known that some units were delivered between 11 May 1944 and 2 May 1945, although their origin remains uncertain. The external appearance of the Sherman IV was very similar to that of the M4A2,

▲ British Sherman immortalised in a street of Francofonte in Sicily on 13/14 July 1943 and belonging to the 13th Armoured Corps of the British 8th Army, engaged in a maximum effort to reach Catania in the shortest possible time. Author's colouring.

▲ British Sherman column during the Italian campaign in a southern Italian village.

▼ Sherman M4 Firefly on display at the tank museum in Bovinton (UK). Courtesy by Geni (Wiki CC3).

Medium tank UK Sherman Mk. II, 10th Royal Hussars, Libya, November 1942.

but the main difference was the engine: it used a powerful 500 hp Ford GAA V8 petrol engine. Other variants existed, such as the Sherman IVA, equipped with the 76 mm M1A2 L/55 gun, and the Sherman IVB, armed with the 105 mm M4 L/22.5 howitzer. A version with HVSS suspension, called the Sherman IVBY, was developed to improve the mobility of the tank.

- **Sherman V**

This model, known as the M4A4, was the most produced Sherman for the British forces, with over 7,000 units produced. Although similar externally to the M4, the hull was slightly longer to accommodate the bulky Chrysler engine. This also required adaptation of the track system, increasing it from 79 to 83 elements per side.

- **Sherman VC (Firefly)**

The Sherman VC, nicknamed 'Firefly', was the most powerful British Sherman model thanks to its 17-pound gun, named after the weight of the projectile. Originally designed as a temporary solution, the Firefly proved extremely effective and quickly became popular among British tanks. Not all Shermans were initially able to handle the new armament, which required complex structural modifications. Eventually, a team of professional engineers solved the technical problems, and the tests exceeded all expectations. Once completed, more than 2,000 Fireflies were ordered. Unfortunately, it was not possible to deploy the Firefly en masse until the Normandy landings; only 342 units were available for D-Day. The name 'Firefly' was chosen under unclear dates and circumstances. In general, all Shermans destined for the UK were modified to improve their efficiency and crew comfort compared to US models.

The Firefly turned out to be (after all) one of the best tanks used by the Allies, 'armed as it was with a superb 17-pounder cannon that finally fired projectiles with initial velocity equal or nearly equal to those of the German Panther and Tiger'!

- **Sherman VI – M4A5**

The designation M4A5 was used for models produced in Canada, known as the Sherman VI.

- **Sherman VII – M4A6**

The M4A6, equipped with the 75mm M3 L/40 gun, featured a composite hull, partly cast and partly welded, and used a new 9-cylinder Ordnance RD-1820 radial diesel engine. Only 75 examples of this model were produced, and there is no record of any of them ever being sent to the UK.

▲ Two Canadian Sherman in the area of Bergen, Holland, 1944.

Medium tank UK Sherman Mk. II, 9th Queen's Royal Lancers, 2nd Armoured Brigade, 1st Division, Egypt, November 1942.

▲ The Canadian Sherman 'Cobalt', belonging to the Three Rivers Regiment, in the streets of Agira, Sicily, July 1943.

▼ British, New Zealand and South African tankers receive instructions from a US technician regarding the use of the Sherman in Egypt in February 1943.

NZ Sherman Mk. II, (M4A1), Warwickshire Yeomanry, 9th Armoured Brigade, 2nd New Zealand Division, December 1942.

OPERATIONAL USE

■ NORTH AFRICAN FRONT

The first Sherman tanks to enter combat in the Second World War were the M4A1 (designated by the British as Sherman II) used by the British Eighth Army in the Second Battle of El Alamein in October 1942. The United States supplied these vehicles quickly, taking them from their own military units and making necessary modifications to adapt them to British requirements and the harsh desert conditions, such as installing sand shields on the tracks.

More than 250 of these American Shermans were distributed among the 12 armoured regiments and successfully participated in the battle. They were organised into 'heavy squadrons' of 16 tanks each, allocated to one brigade of each division of the 10th Armoured Corps, with additional squadrons assigned to other units in the field. Other 'heavy squadrons' were at that time still equipped with M3 Lee/Grant tanks, while the 'light squadrons' had M3 Stuart and Crusader tanks.

British Shermans proved to be effective against enemy rear and defence troops due to their high explosive (HE) shells, which were used to indirectly hit the enemy. The German 5 cm Pak 38 anti-tank gun could only penetrate the Sherman's armour if it could attack it on the weaker sides. The success of the Sherman at the Battle of El Alamein led many British armoured units in North Africa to gradually increase the number of these vehicles, adding the Sherman III (M4A2) models along with the earlier Sherman IIs. However, armoured infantry units continued to mainly use their old Churchill tanks.

▲ The British Sherman with the inscription 'A merry Christmas' neatly painted on the camouflage hull, in the Libyan desert in the Benghazi area on 26 December 1942.

Medium tank UK Sherman Mk. III (M4A2) The Queen's Bay, 2nd Armoured Brigade, 1st Armored Division, 1942.

THE CAMPAIGN IN ITALY OF THE BRITISH FORCES

The British forces in Italy did not employ their usual tanks like the Crusader. Instead, they almost completely replaced these with Sherman tanks and Stuart turretless light vehicles, equipped with a standard cannon, for reconnaissance operations. Another tank used in the campaign was the Churchill, initially equipped with a 6-pounder gun and, in later versions, with a 75 mm main gun; these armoured units were, however, heavily supplemented by Shermans. Typically, Shermans were used as infantry support to overcome rough terrain and to tackle static German defences and fortifications, especially in mountainous and hilly areas. Towards the end of 1944, the British also began to deploy enhanced versions of the Sherman, armed with 76-mm guns, 105-mm howitzers and 17-pounders, to counter the defences of the Gothic Line, which was built and fortified by the Germans.

THE NORMANDY LANDINGS AND THE CAMPAIGN IN FRANCE

British and Commonwealth forces' use of the Sherman in Europe was equally extensive. The Sherman almost completely replaced the M3 Grant and Lee tanks, as well as the Ram tank in service with the Canadian Army, becoming by far the most common vehicle in early 1944. The other main British tanks at the end of the war were the Churchill and the Cromwell: the Cromwell was mainly used for reconnaissance, while the Churchill, slower but with thicker armour, was intended for armoured infantry support brigades.

The 17-pounder Sherman version was mainly produced by modifying the M4 Sherman I and M4A4 Sherman V, with some units also based on the Sherman III, and provided the Sherman and Cromwell

▲ British Sherman Firefly at Namur, 1944. This is a composite M4, showing a cast hull front with large crew hatches.

▲ A Polish Sherman reinforced with sandbags, Cassino area, Italy. May 1944.

▲ Il Major-General canadese Hoffmeister, fotografato a bordo di uno Sherman, Italia 1944.

Medium tank UK Sherman Mk. III, 'Abdiel', 3rd County of London Yeomanry, August 1943.

Medium tank UK Sherman Mk. III, 'Sheik', The Royal Scots Grey (2nd Dragoons), Italy, September 1943.

armoured units with increased anti-tank capability. The production of the Cromwell armed 17-pounder proved insufficient, necessitating the use of Sherman VCs, produced in larger numbers, as reinforcements. A British armoured squadron in 1944 (equivalent to an American company) had one 17-pounder Sherman for every platoon of four Shermans.

The 17-pounder Sherman remained in Cromwell units until the arrival of the Comet tank, equipped with a 77 mm HV cannon. This gun, derived from the 17-pounder, used 17-pounder projectiles in a reduced cartridge of the now obsolete 3-inch 20 cwt anti-aircraft gun, offering less recoil and slightly less penetration.

By the end of the war, about 50 per cent of the Shermans in UK service were VC or IC versions. With the conclusion of the conflict and the introduction of more advanced tanks, the UK returned Shermans to the US in an attempt to reduce Lend-Lease costs.

However, the United States was not interested in the return of Shermans modified with the 17-pounder cannon to their stores, and many of these tanks were transferred from British reserves to other armies after the war, remaining in service in some countries until the 1960s. One example was the Argentine 'Repotenciado' upgrade of the Sherman IC and VC, equipped with a 105 mm French gun and diesel engine.

SHERMAN'S MILITARY INTERVENTIONS OF OTHER COUNTRIES

India

In the Indian Army tradition, the formations included both British regiments and Indian Army units. Besides some Indian units receiving Sherman tanks, the 116th Regiment of the Royal Armoured Corps (converted from the 9th Battalion of the Gordon Highlanders), belonging to the 255th Brigade, was also

▲ An amphibious DD (Duplex Drive) Sherman with waterproof protection. Once in the water, the buoyant screen was raised and the rear propellers came into operation.

equipped with Shermans. In January and February 1945, these mixed forces as part of the 255th brigade were engaged in Burma in operations near Meiktila and Mandalay. In these actions, the tanks were mainly used for infantry support, with few direct clashes with enemy tanks. Later, they were part of the mobile columns that moved to recapture Rangoon.

New Zealand

The 4th New Zealand Armoured Brigade used around 150 M4A2 Sherman tanks from late 1942 until the end of the war. This brigade, part of the 2nd New Zealand Division, had been converted from an infantry brigade and actively participated in the Italian Campaign.

Australia

In 1942, the Australian Army received 757 M3 Lee/Grant tanks, but only three Shermans, supplied by the United Kingdom. In early 1944, the War Office asked the Australian Army to test the Churchill and Sherman tanks in conditions similar to those in New Guinea. Trials were conducted in jungle terrain, using British Churchill Mk IV, Mk V and Mk VII infantry tanks and American Sherman M4A1 and M4A2 Medium tanks. The first Australian M4A2 Sherman arrived in 1943, followed by two more M4s (sometimes incorrectly referred to as M4A1s) for tropical trials in New Guinea in 1944. These tanks were entrusted to crews of the Australian 4th Armoured Brigade. However, for the operational terrain in which they were intended to fight, the Shermans proved less suitable than the Churchills. After the conflict, the three test Shermans were displayed on Australian military bases and one of them was later destroyed after being used as a target in tests.

▲ A Polish Sherman near the Dutch town of Moerdijkil 10 November 1944.

Medium tank UK Sherman Mk. III, 5th Royal Tank Regiment, Naples, late 1943.

Canada

The United States did not officially consider Canada a beneficiary of the Lend-Lease programme, but in 1941, through subsequent agreements, Canada was allowed to produce some variants of the M4A1. In all, Canada received four Shermans through Lend-Lease. Instead, MLW manufactured 188 Sherman tanks named Grizzly I for the Canadian Army, but these were only intended for training purposes. As US production capacity was sufficient, MLW diverted its Ram and Sherman tank production efforts to the construction of Sexton self-propelled guns, equipped with 25-pound howitzers mounted on M3 or M4 chassis. On the European front, the Canadian forces used American Shermans supplied by the UK, armed with 75 mm, 105 mm and 17-pounder guns.

China

Chinese forces stationed in British India received 100 Sherman M4A4s from the British reserves, using them with great success against Japanese tanks, which were of much inferior quality, and against enemy infantry during several offensives, such as those in the Battle of Northern Burma and Western Yunnan between 1943 and 1944. In total, it is estimated that China received around 812 Shermans through the Lend-Lease. After the war, some of these vehicles that remained in India were given to the British, while many others were used by the Chinese Nationalists (Kuomintang or KMT) against Communist forces during the Chinese Civil War, until the KMT's defeat in 1949.

Soviet Union

The M4A2s supplied to the Red Army were considered less prone to explosions due to detonation of ammunition than the T-34s, but had a greater tendency to roll over in road accidents, collisions or over uneven terrain due to their higher centre of gravity. In the context of the Lend-Lease, the Soviet Union received over 4,000 M4A2 medium tanks, of which 2,000 were equipped with the original 75 mm cannon and 2,095 with the more powerful 76 mm cannon. The first diesel M4A2s with 76 mm cannon arrived in

▲ Soviet M4A2 Sherman of the 8th Guards Mechanized Corps at Grabow in Germany, May 1945.

the Soviet Union in the late summer of 1944. In 1945, a number of Soviet armoured units began to rely mainly on these Shermans instead of the T-34s, including the 1st and 3rd Guard Mechanised Corps, the 6th Guard Armoured Army and the 9th Guard Mechanised Corps. The Sherman enjoyed a good reputation among many Soviet crews that had used it, due to its reliability, ease of maintenance, firepower (especially the 76 mm gun version) and adequate armour protection.

Poland

Poland did not receive Lend-Lease aid directly from the United States, but Polish forces still had access to a wide range of Sherman tanks from Lend-Lease supplies destined for the United Kingdom. The Polish 1st Armoured Division took part in the Battle of Normandy with equipment consisting mainly of Sherman V (M4A4) tanks with 75 mm guns and VC Sherman. After the heavy losses suffered in the closing of the Falaise pocket and the campaign in Holland, the division was resupplied with new tanks, mainly Sherman IIA (M4A1 (W) 76 mm) models.

The Polish II Corps, engaged in Italy, mainly used M4A2 (Sherman III) tanks already used by the British Army in Africa, although some IC tanks and Sherman IB howitzers (M4 105 mm) were employed. Some units of the Polish First Army temporarily used M4A2s (76 mm) borrowed from the Soviet army after the heavy losses suffered in the conquest of Danzig. After receiving new supplies, the army was then equipped with T-34 tanks.

France

The first use of Sherman tanks by a French unit dates back to the 1st Compagnie Autonome de Chars de Combat (1st CACC), which joined the French Army Corps Reconnaissance Group (GRCA) and was nicknamed the 'Flying Column of Free Frenchmen'. This unit, part of the British Eighth Army, fought from the Battle of El Alamein to Tunisia. The company was later assigned to 'Force L (Leclerc)' and became the

▲ M4A3(76) Sherman 'Champagne' tank of the French 2nd Armoured Division, which was hit on 13 September 1944 and is still stored in Ville-sur-Illon, near Dompaire.

▲ View of the British M4 Sherman tank from above.

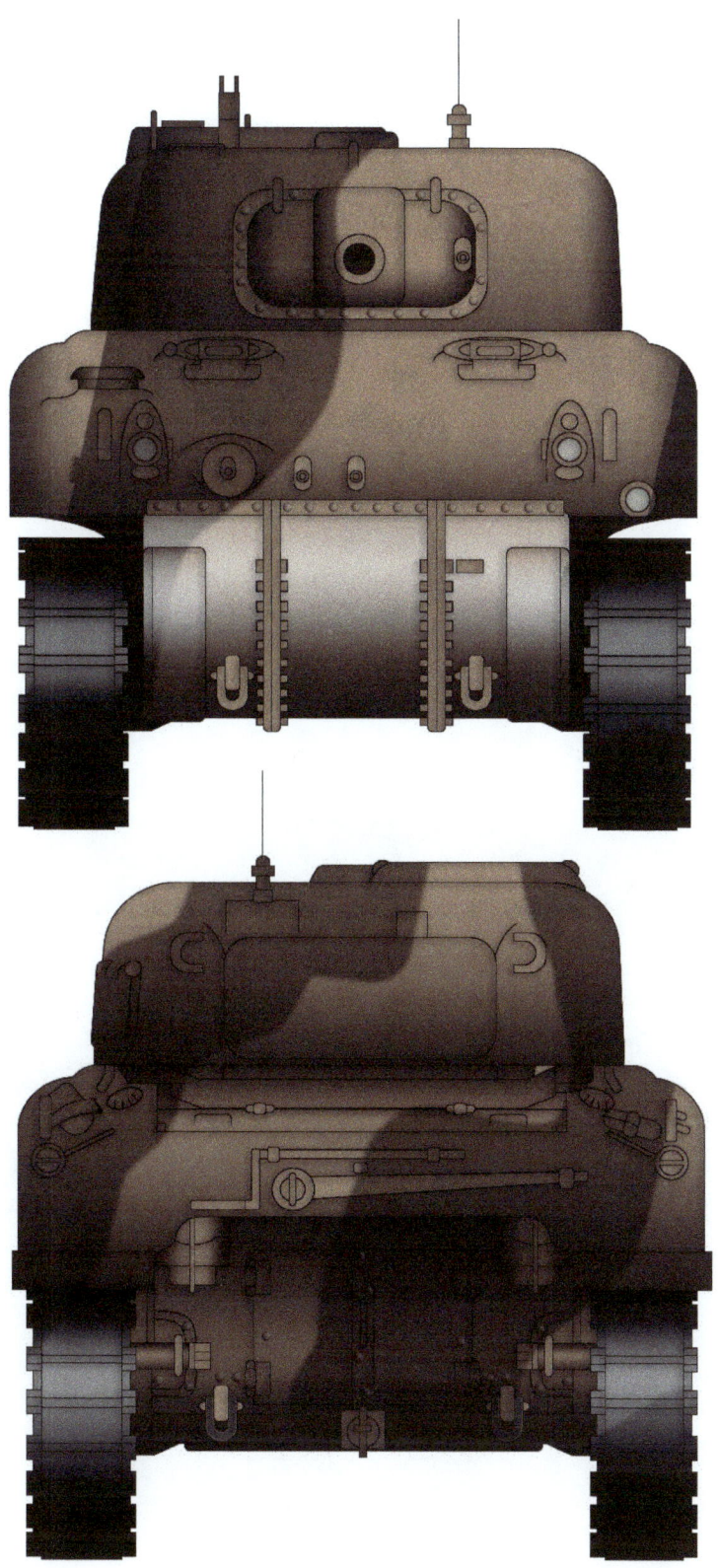

▲ Front and rear view of the British M4 Sherman tank.

Medium tank UK Sherman Mk. I, 79th Armoured Division, Great Britain, March 1944.

1st Company of the 501st Fighter Tank Regiment in the newly formed 2nd Armoured Division. In 1943, the Free French Forces decided to establish a new army in North Africa and reached an agreement with the United States to receive modern military equipment. France thus obtained 656 Sherman tanks through the Lend-Lease programme (274 M4A4s and 362 M4A2s, plus 20 reconditioned M4A2s), becoming the third largest recipient of these vehicles.

The French armoured divisions were structured according to the organisation chart of the US 'light' armoured divisions of 1943, with 165 Shermans per division. The French 2nd Armoured Division (Division Blindée, DB) participated in the Battle of Normandy fully equipped with M4A2s. The 1st and 5th DB, which landed in southern France with the French First Army, were equipped with a combination of M4A2 and M4A4 tanks.

Later, the French also received M4A3(76) and M4A3(75)W models as replacements for their losses, as well as a number of M4A3(105). The 2nd DB obtained some M4(105) as early as late July 1944, while still in the UK. The 3rd DB, used as a training and reserve unit for the other three operational armoured divisions, possessed around 200 medium and light tanks, 120 of which were later transferred to the US Army's Delta Base Section in Marseille for redeployment. Towards the end of the war in Europe, French units also received some M4A1(75) rebuilt in the US and sent to Europe.

▲ An amphibious Sherman DD tank of the 13th/18th Royal Hussars in action against German troops. Normandy 1944.

Brazil

In 1944, Brazil received 53 Sherman tanks through the Lend-Lease programme, all armed with 75 mm cannon. These tanks were not used by the Brazilian Expeditionary Force in Italy, but remained at home for the defence of Brazil. In the early 1950s, Brazil received another 30 Shermans through the Military Assistance Programme, bringing the total to 83 tanks. Among them were 40 M4s, 38 M4 composite-hulled and 2 M4A1s. The Brazilian Army used Shermans until 1979, when they were replaced by M41 tanks.

Czechoslovakia

The Czechoslovak government-in-exile did not receive direct supplies from the United States, but the 1st Czechoslovak Armoured Brigade was nonetheless equipped by the British army. During the siege of Dunkirk, the brigade had 36 Sherman ICs, in addition to Cromwell tanks, which constituted the brigade's main armoured vehicle. In May 1945, Shermans armed with a 17-pound gun were exchanged for 22 Challenger tanks, with which the brigade returned home. In addition, a damaged Sherman I tank, abandoned by an unknown unit, was recovered from the battlefield and used by the brigade as a recovery vehicle, returning to Czechoslovakia with the same brigade.

South Africa

The Sherman tanks supplied to South Africa were used by the 6th Armoured Division.

▲ Sherman and Cromwell tanks of the Royal Marines Armoured Support Group near Tilly-sur-Seulles during the Normandy campaign in the summer of 1944.

Medium tank UK Sherman Mk. II A, Queen's Bays (2nd Dragoon Guards), November 1944.

Medium tank UK Sherman Mk. IIA, C Squadron, Special Service Battalion, 11th South African Armoured Brigade, Italy, spring 1945.

CAMOUFLAGE AND DISTINCTIVE SIGNS

The background colours and camouflage tints of British military vehicles (AFVs) during the Second World War were determined by a series of Army Council (ACI) instructions and poured onto military training pamphlets (MTP), with specific general orders (GO) used in the Middle East. The paint was supplied to the units pre-mixed (PFU prepared for use) corresponding to two British standards: BS381C from 1930 and BS987C from 1942-45.

Contemporary photographs and the testimonies of veterans confirm that, with a few slight variations, these orders were mostly strictly adhered to but, as far as the models used were concerned, there were sometimes slight variations. The regulations, for example, provided for immediate application of the new standards, however, even to exhaust old paint stocks, the old colour was often opted for

This led to the appearance of very curious colourings at times, often with interesting results involving all four basic colours.

■ EUROPEAN AND METROPOLITAN THEATRE COLOURS

Immediately after the end of the First World War, vehicles and AFVs continued to be painted as in 1914-18. In the 1920s, various colours were used, mainly the discounted browns, greens and greys. Officially these were called 'service colours', which are difficult to establish today.

However, in the early 1930s these colours were mainly a light khaki or greenish ochre.

The interiors of the vehicles were always a silver colour from the 1930s until around mid-1940, when glossy white was used for all. Soon after, and at least until early 1939, the service colour became a glossy *deep bronze green*.

In the first two years of the war, and more precisely from 1939 to 1941, horizontal/diagonal patterns of two different types of green were practised on military vehicles. The usual basic colour was khaki green with a dark green breaker called No. 4, or rarely light green No. 5, and alternatively *green 3*.

From the mid-1940s *dark tarmac* began to replace the two greens No. 4 and 5. Apparently, this choice was motivated by the need to preserve stocks of chromium oxide, an element needed to produce strong colours and a certain degree of infrared immunity. Between 1941 and 1942, the British standard camouflage colours (SCC) of the second British standard came into use until, once the old paint stocks were exhausted, both greens and *dark tarmac* were supplanted.

However, shortages in supply and availability, caused by the scarcity of green pigment, caused the basic colour to be changed in many cases to brown, which in turn was darkened by a dark brown or alternatively black.

In the 1942-44 period, the diagrams introduced a new two-tone pattern using browns as per the regulations. The most common camouflage versions at the time were the *'foliage'* and/or *'dapple'* pattern. In June 1943, the 1° Canadian Corps was instructed to repaint all vehicles in the basic *light stone* or *Portland stone* colour, with various areas of disturbance at the bottom of the body and cabin in black.

This was before deployment to North Africa to take part in Operation Husky in July 1943. The repainting included the addition of clear roundels on the roof to help the RAF recognise friendly vehicles.

In 1944-45, there was a switch to the use of *olive drab* as the new base colour, in order to eliminate the need to repaint US-supplied vehicles. From August 1944, therefore, except on vehicles already painted under the old regulations, *olive drab* became the formal base colour.

During the Italian campaign of 1943, many vehicles used the above-mentioned schemes, but others were painted according to the African-Middle Eastern scheme that used a base colour of *'light mud'* with bold black or dark olive green patterns.

Many of these vehicles were then repainted and, eventually, most of the British vehicle fleet was standardised with the basic *olive drab* coating.

WW2 BRITISH TANK COLORS & CAMOUFLAGE

- Silver Grey — Afrika-Balkan
- Slate — Afrika-Balkan
- Light Stone — Afrika-Balkan
- Portland Stone — Afrika-Balkan
- Desert Pink — Afrika-Balkan
- Dark Olive — Afrika-Balkan
- Dark Gun Metal
- Olive Drab — Disruptive Europe
- Blue Black — Disruptive Europe
- Light Mud — Disruptive Europe
- Brown — Disruptive Europe
- Dark Brown — Disruptive Europe
- Deep Bronze Green — Disruptive Europe
- Tommy Green

MIDDLE EASTERN AND AFRICAN THEATRE COLOURS

In July 1939, the regulations for this strategic sector specified a basic tone called *middle stone* with variations of *'dark sand'*. The tanks of the 6th RTC A9 began to use the *stone* hue and in May 1940 added dark sand patches. This scheme became common in Egypt in the summer of 1940. In 1940-41 the vehicles were painted in three tones of *light stone* or *Portland stone* as a base colour with diagonal stripes and additions of *silver grey* and *slate* or *green* 3 used in different variations. One scheme used in Sudan had light stone or *Portland stone* with light brown-purple instead of silver grey, and *light stone* No. 61 instead of slate for the same model.

The two-tone pattern based on 'Caunter' and used in Greece in April and May 1941 was obtained by using *light stone* or *slate* or some other unknown colour. Light violet-brown, in short, was used exclusively in Sudan. In December 1941 the use of the two *stone* colours was still imposed, but only a possible third colour was added for camouflage. At first it appeared that slate-coloured camouflage was chosen, but later more and more vehicles with green or silver-grey camouflage or even brown were noticed. Various departments and brigades strove to choose a camouflage that would distinguish them from each other. This continued until October 1942, when a Camcolor range of water-based colours was developed for all camouflage purposes.

From October 1942 a new counterorder: all previous designs were cancelled to be replaced by new standardised designs for certain AFV types and vehicle classes.

The new colours that appeared on the horizon were a basic tone of *desert pink* with a disruptive pattern in *dark olive green*. Black, very dark brown and dark slate were the alternative variables.

These new patterns began to appear on Shermans, Grants, Valentines, Crusaders, and Stuarts; while Churchill tanks, painted in the UK with *light stone*, featured a red-brown pattern in the Crusader motif. Since *desert pink* was a new colour, *light stone* continued to be used on existing vehicles. *Desert pink* was then used alone as a single tone on vehicles without tactical value. From April 1943, the regulation was once again cancelled and new models issued with new colours for use in Tunisia, Sicily, Italy and throughout the Middle East. The basic tone became *'light mud'* with black or other in bold patterns used for camouflage. By 1944, European colours and patterns also predominated in vehicles in the Middle East.

FAR EASTERN COLOURS

Until 1943, the vehicles appear to have conformed to UK standards. There are colour pictures of military vehicles in Singapore in *khaki green* and *dark tarmac*. In early 1943, *jungle green* was introduced to be used as the only general colour. But in 1944, *dark drab* also appeared. In 1944, there was a range of colours for camouflage purposes issued by SEAC in Ceylon (now Sri Lanka), but there is no evidence that any of these were intended as a disruptive colour. From 1943 to 1945 there was only one general base colour.

Sherman Medium Tank V. A Squadron, 11th Armoured Regiment (The Ontario Regiment), 1st Canadian Armoured Brigade, Sicily, Italy, August 1943.

▲▼ British Sherman in the Normandy landings. June 1944.

Sherman Medium Tank V. A Squadron, 14th Armoured Regiment (The Calgary Regiment), 1st Canadian Armoured Brigade, Italy, September 1943.

Sherman V medium tank, Divisional headquarters, 5th Canadian Armoured Division, Italy, late 1944.

CAMOUFLAGE SPECIFICATIONS AND MARKS

The typical marking for British Shermans and tanks was to identify each squadron within a regiment. This system involved the use of empty geometric shapes: a diamond for HQ, a triangle for A Squadron, a square for B Squadron and a circle for C Squadron. In regiments that also had a D Squadron, a solid coloured rectangle was used. Within the brigade, the seniority of the regiments was represented by the colour of the insignia: red for the oldest regiment, yellow for the second and blue for the youngest. These insignia were always painted on the turret sides, sides and front of the hull, and also on the back of the hull.

In theory, the symbol of one's division or brigade was mandatory, however, many tanks deployed in North Africa and Italy did not display such badges.

Then next to or in combination with the formation badge, the divisional unit number, also known as the Arm of Service (AoS) marking, was also displayed.

In June 1942, an air recognition marking was introduced in the shape of a circle, similar to that of the Royal Air Force, a system also used for Italian armour in Africa. This mark could reach a maximum diameter of 150cm, but could be scaled down to fit the available surface area while still respecting the

▲ Sherman of the 8th Armoured Brigade at Kevelaer, Germany 4 March 1945.

original proportions. On the Sherman, this marking was usually visible on the rear of the hull and/or on the turret roof. It is important to note that neither the colours nor the proportions were RAF colours: instead, bright shades of yellow, red and blue were used. In April 1944, this marking was replaced in all theatres of operation by the five-pointed star within a circle.

CAMOUFLAGE

The first Sherman tanks to arrive in North Africa, official camouflage instructions required the vehicles to be painted in a basic colour known as 'Desert Yellow,' a light tone similar to sand yellow. At that time, the choice to apply additional camouflage schemes was left to the unit command, often at brigade level, and many regiments were distinguishable by the particular camouflage scheme applied to their tanks. However, for security reasons, an order issued in October 1942 cancelled these provisions and imposed standard camouflage schemes for certain vehicle categories. The new authorised basic colour was 'Desert Pink Z.I.,' and camouflage designs were to be made in Dark Green (Olive). If this was not available, alternatives such as black, very dark brown or dark slate could be used. 'Desert Pink' was produced locally and described as a warm, sandy shade of pink.

This order remained in force, with some modifications, until April 1943, when new directives and schemes were issued in view of the operations in Sicily and Italy. The basic colour was changed to a tone of 'Light Mud', with contrasting patterns in black or dark green. Vehicles coming from the United States and painted in the standard colour 'Olive Drab' No. 9 were to receive a camouflage layer of 'Light Mud'. Schemes with a light mud base and a dark contrasting colour were observed on tanks in Italy until 1944. This scheme was intended for the entire Middle East Command, and there is no evidence of the use of a sand and red scheme reported for Egypt and Syria in late 1942 and early 1943.

In the UK, the standard base colour was known as SCC 2 or 'Service Colour', a dark brown with a slight khaki tint, while black was permitted for contrasting purposes. In April 1944, a new colour called SCC 15 Olive Drab was introduced, making it unnecessary to repaint American vehicles, which were now left with their original US Army 'Olive Drab' colour.

In August 1944, the use of contrasting motifs was definitively discontinued for all vehicles.

▲ A Canadian Sherman tank, the famous Grizzly, preserved in the Heeresgeschichtliches Museum in Wien.

French Sherman III medium tank, 8th HQ Armoured Brigade, France, June 1944.

Polish Medium Tank, Sherman of the Polish 1st Armoured Division.

Sherman M4A2(76) W. 1st Polish Medium Tank Corps. Berlin, April 1945.

APPENDIX

The German Tiger heavy tank was a formidable machine, capable of dominating European battlefields. Among the most feared weapon systems of the Second World War, it had the reputation of being invincible, a myth that was only shattered with the arrival of the British Sherman Firefly in the summer of 1944. This tank, designed by the British specifically to counter the Tiger, was based on the American Sherman M4A4 but equipped with a powerful 17-pound (76.2 mm) cannon, which made it extremely effective in combat.

This vehicle had its moment of glory on 8 August 1944 when the new armoured vehicle, during a famous battle, handed victory to the Anglo-Americans thanks to their numerical, tactical and engineering superiority. We are talking about Operation Totalize in which the German super ace Wittmann lost his life, along with four members of his crew, after destroying a total of 139 tanks during the course of the war. All by the Firefly at Saint-Aignan-de-Cramesnil.

There are several theories regarding his death: some claim that his tank was shot down by a Sherman Firefly of the 33rd Armoured Brigade, while other sources indicate that the tank was hit by a rocket fired from a Hawker Typhoon.

More recent studies by US historians have confirmed that Wittmann advanced with his Tiger 007 together with three other tanks from his unit. The Yeomanry's British Firefly, which was about 700 metres to the side, destroyed the three tanks, but not Wittmann's, which was 1000 metres away, a distance that would have been too long for the Firefly. However, there is a photograph of the wreckage which shows that Tiger 007 was hit on the left flank, at the rear; this fact exonerates the rocket thesis and corroborates the hit by the Firefly or similar Canadian Sherbrookes tanks present during the battle!

DATA SHEET	
	Sherman III (M4A2) UK 🇬🇧
Length	5920 mm
Width	2620 mm
Height	2740 mm
Date of entry into service/exit	April 1942 to May 1945
Weight in combat order	29,94 t
Crew	5 (commander, pilot, servants and gunner)
Engine	General Motors 6046 diesel 410 CV (310 kW)
Maximum speed	48 km/h on road 30 km/h off strada
Autonomy	240 km on road, 180 off strada
Suspension	Vertical Volute Spring Suspension (VVSS)
Armour	13 to 108mm
Armament	1 M3 L/40 75 mm gun with 97 rounds 1 Browning M2HB cal. 50 machine gun 2 Browning M1919A4 cal .30 (7.62 mm) machine guns
Production	5.000

Sherman Vc 'Firefly' Polish 1st Armoured Division medium tank, 1945.

▲ Soviet Sherman in the Křenov-Straße in Brno (Czechoslovakia) in April 1945.

▲ British Sherman III and VC of the 8th Armored Brigade at Kevelaer in Germany, March 4, 1945.

Russian M4A2(75)W medium tank of the 46th Armoured Brigade, 1st Armoured Division, Northern Front, winter 1943-44.

Russian Sherman M4A2 medium tank, from an unknown unit. Leningrad, Winter Frenzy 1943-1944.

Russian Sherman M4A2(76) W medium tank. Of the 9th Guard Tank Brigade, 1st USSR Mechanised Corps Austria, spring 1945.

BIBLIOGRAPHY

- Bishop, Chris *The Encyclopedia of Weapons of World War II* (2002) Metro Books.
- Calderon e Fernandez, *Sherman the American miracle*, spain 2017
- Chamberlain, Peter; Ellis, Chris. *British and American Tanks of World War II*. New York: Arco.
- Culver B. *"Sherman in Action"*, Squadron/Signal Publications, 1977.
- Doyle David, *Sherman Tank: America's M4 and M4, 105, Medium Tanks in World War II*
- Esteve Michel, Sherman: *The M4 Tank in World War II* Casematte pubblisher
- Fletcher D., *"Sherman Firefly"*, Osprey Publishing Ltd., 2008.
- Ford Roger, *The Sherman Tank: Weapons of War* , History press UK
- Forty G. *"United States Tanks of World War II"*, Blandford Press, 1989.
- Gawrych Wojcisch, *M4A2 Sherman Part 1*. Armor photogallery
- Gawrych Wojcisch, *M4 Sherman WC Firefly*. Armor photogallery
- Askew Michael, *M4 Sherman Tanks: The Illustrated History of America's Most Iconic Fighting Vehicles*
- Hunnicutt, R. P. Sherman, *A History of the American Medium Tank*. 1978; Taurus Enterprises.
- Mesko J., *"Walk Around M4 Sherman"*, Squadron/Signal Publications, 2000.
- Mokva Stanislaw, *M4 Sherman: M4, M4A1, M4A4 Firefly*, Kagero
- Oliver Dennis, *British Sherman tanks 1944-1945*
- Oliver Dennis, *British armor in Sicily and Italy 1944-1945*
- Oliver Dennis, *Sherman tanks US army in Europe 1944-1945*
- Porter, David *Allied Tanks of World War II (World's Great Weapons)* (2014) Amber Books
- Sandars J. *"The Sherman Tank in British Service 1942-45"*, Osprey Publishing, 1982.
- Stansell P., Laughlin K., *"Son of Sherman Vol. 1: The Sherman Design and Development"*, The Ampersand Group, 2013.
- USMC D-F Series Tables of Equipment (TOEs), 1942-1944.
- White B. T., *"British Tanks and Fighting Vehicles 1914-1945"* Ian Allan Ltd., 1970.
- War departement, *M4 Sherman Medium Tank Crew Manual*
- Ware Pat, *M4 Sherman: Entwicklung, Technik, Einsatz*
- Ware Pat, *Char Sherman: Toutes les variantes du M4 depuis 1941*
- Zaloga, Steven (2008). *Armored Thunderbolt: The US Army Sherman in World War II*. Stackpole Books. ISBN 978-0-8117-0424-3.
- Zaloga S. J., *"M4 (76mm) Sherman Medium Tank 1943-65"*, Osprey Publishing, 2003.
- Zaloga S. J., *"Patton's Tanks"*, Arms and Armour Press, 1984
- Zaloga S. J., *"Sherman Medium Tank 1942-1945"*, Osprey Publishing, 1993.
- Zaloga S. J., *The Sherman at war, US army in Europe* Concord Publishing.

ALREADY PUBLISHED TITLES

ALL BOOKS IN THE SERIES ARE PRINTED IN ITALIAN AND ENGLISH

VISIT OUR WEBSITE FOR MORE INFORMATION ON
THE WEAPONS ENCYCLOPAEDIA:
https://soldiershop.com/collane/libri/the-weapons-encyclopaedia/

TWE-031 EN

www.ingramcontent.com/pod-product-compliance
Lightning Source LLC
LaVergne TN
LVHW072122060526
838201LV00068B/4947